RAMBAM
his life and times

Student Workbook
Level ה

by Brenda Bacon

edited by Marcia Kaunfer
and Eduardo Rauch

student activities and exercises
designed and illustrated by Nina Woldin

curriculum supervision by Seymour Fox

THE MELTON RESEARCH CENTER
of The Jewish Theological Seminary of America

Published by The Melton Research Center
of The Jewish Theological Seminary of America
3080 Broadway, New York, N.Y. 10027
(212) 678-8031

MANUFACTURED IN THE UNITED STATES OF AMERICA

This Melton Center curriculum project
has been made possible by
a generous grant from the
Maurice Amado Foundation.

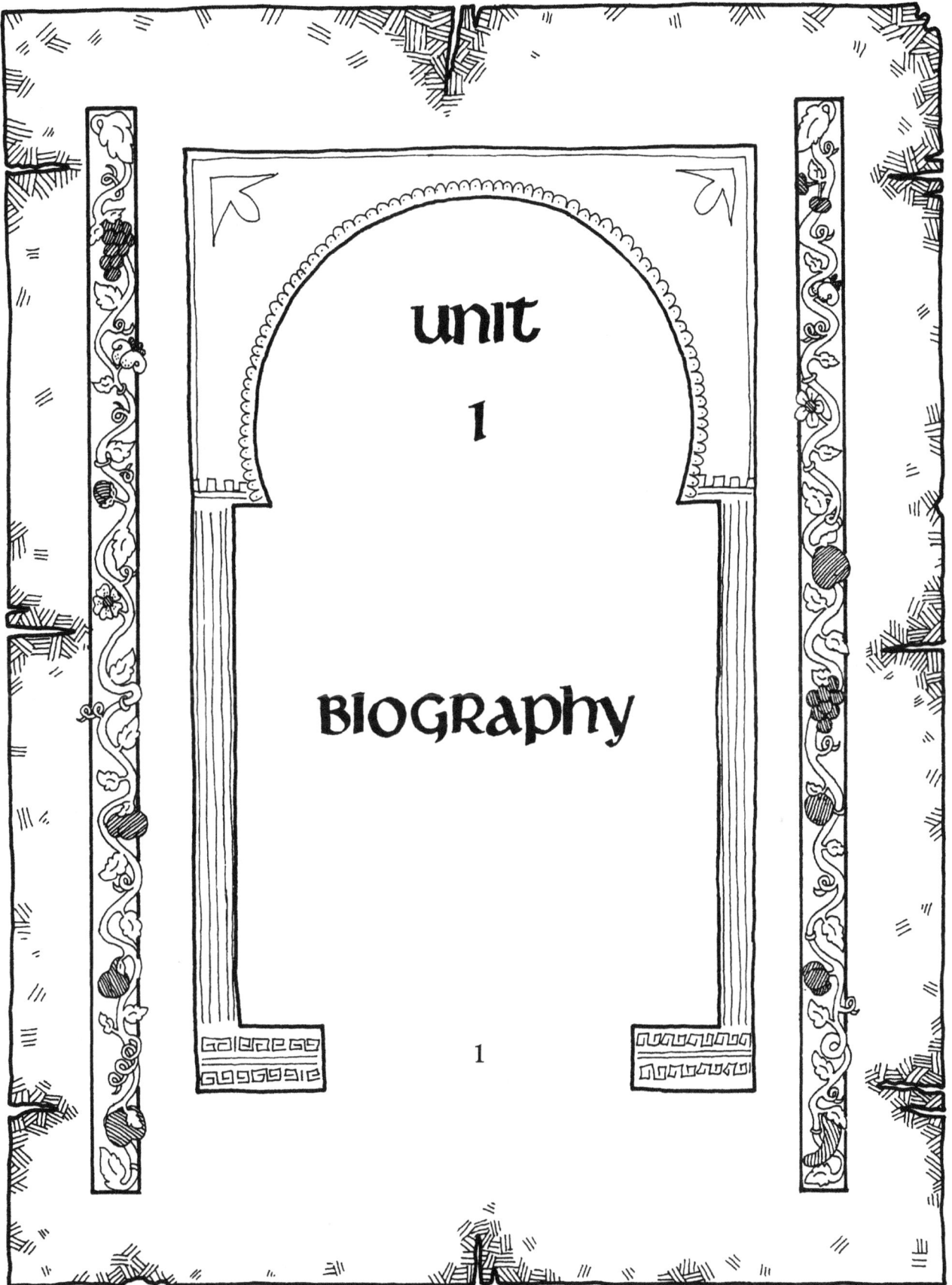

UNIT 1

BIOGRAPHY

my name is...

any famous rabbis became known by the first initials of their names. For example, Rabbi Moshe ben Maimon became known as Rambam (רמב״ם), and Rabbi Levi ben Gershon was known as Ralbag, (רלב״ג).

Use this worksheet to find out what your name would be if you were a rabbi.

Fill in the spaces below, putting the first letter of your answer in the circle.

Rabbi _____ ב ⓡ

My first name in Hebrew is: _____ ◯

Son/daughter of: ת ⓑ / ⓑ

My father's/mother's first
name in Hebrew is: _____ ◯

If I were a famous rabbi known by the first initials of my names, my name would be:
_____ _____ _____ _____ (copy the four letters circled here.)

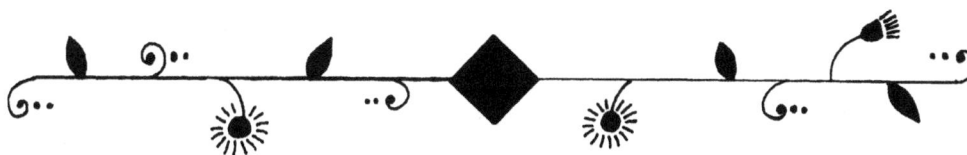

RAMBAM'S FAMILY TREE

OBADIA
↓
RABBI SOLOMON
↓
OBADIA THE DAYAN *
↓
JOSEPH THE DAYAN *
↓
JOSEPH THE LEARNED
↓
MAIMON THE DAYAN *
↓
MOSES 1135–1204

*JUDGE

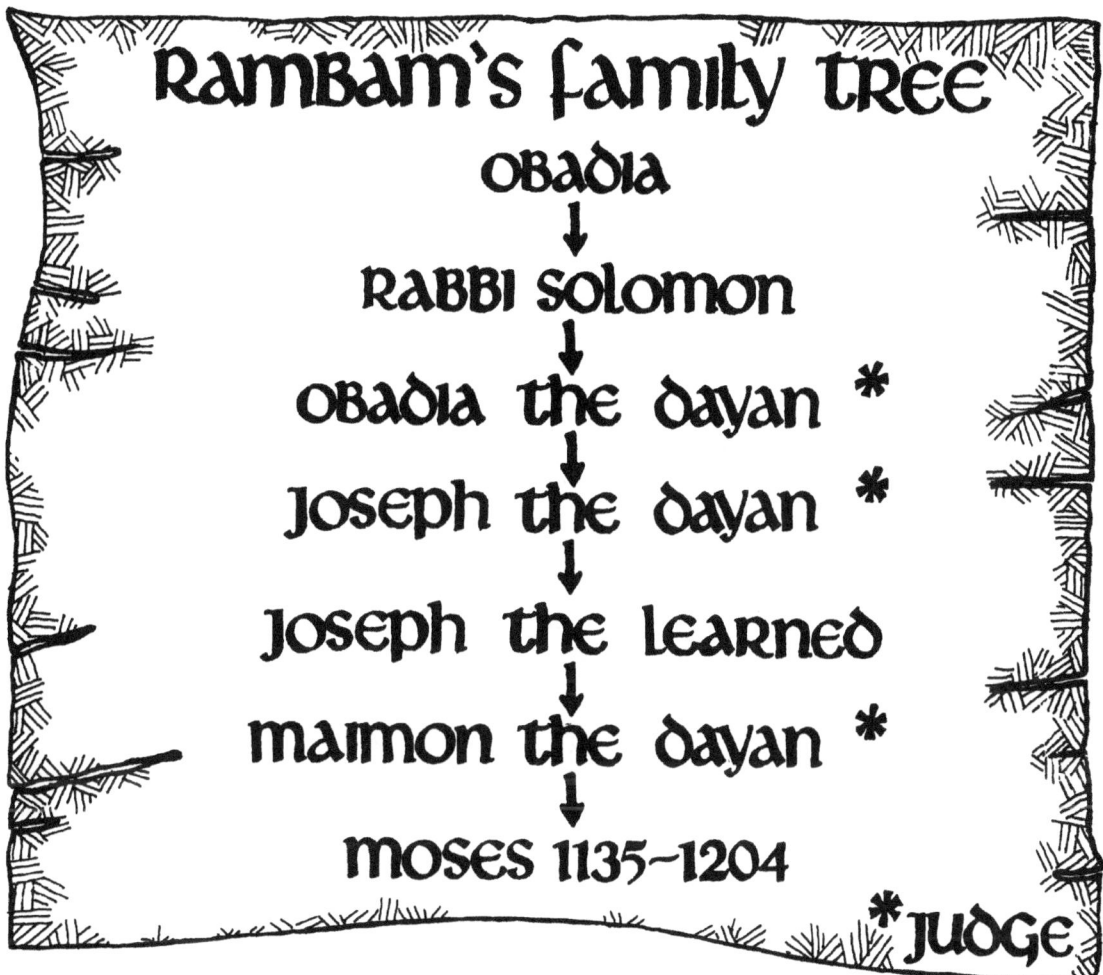

This is what we know about Moses Maimonides' family, according to what he wrote in his commentary to the Mishnah. Moses Maimonides even had a tradition that he was descended from Rabbi Judah the Prince, who lived in the latter half of the second and first half of the third century C.E.

my family tree

Fill in your family tree on this grid. Whenever possible put English and Hebrew names.

_____ _____ _____ _____
Your father's father   Your father's mother   Your mother's father   Your mother's mother

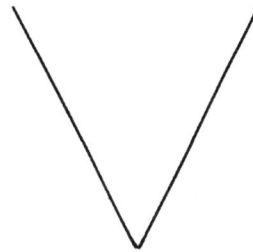

_____   _____
Your father   Your mother

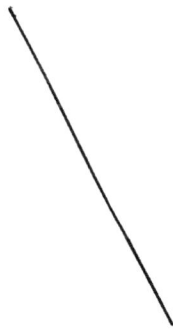

_____ _____ _____ _____ _____
Your brother   Your brother   You   Your brother   Your brother
or sister   or sister   or sister   or sister

If you Ran your school...

... which subjects would be studied?

Fill in each column below. Tell why you have chosen each subject that would be taught
in your school. How many courses would you have in Jewish studies? Why?

RAMBAM STUDIED:	YOU ACTUALLY STUDY:	YOUR SCHOOL WOULD TEACH:
Torah, Mishnah & Hebrew grammar		
Poetry		
Talmud		
Philosophic observations on religion		
Philosophic studies		
Logic		
Mathematics		
Geometry		
Optics		
Astronomy		
Physics		
Natural sciences		
Metaphysics		

5

Today Hugh Argue will interview a Moslem and a Jew. How do you think they will answer these questions?

What do you think about each of the following laws?

___ ". . . The lives and property of non-Moslems are protected in exchange for the payments a of head tax . . ."

___ ". . . Jews must wear clothes identifying them as non-Moslems . . ."

___ ". . . Jews cannot build new synagogues or enlarge old ones . . ."

___ ". . . Jewish courts have no authority over Moslems . . ."

___ ". . . Jews may use the same bath houses as Moslems and Christians . . ."

Now, number the laws from one to five, from the most harmful, to the least harmful to Jews.

meet the leaders

Suppose the leaders of the Jewish community in medieval times could visit your community today, and speak to its leaders. How would medieval Jewish leaders answer these questions? How would the leaders of your community answer these questions?

1. How do you collect the money to support your community? _____

_____

_____

2. Is there any pressure on the Jews in your community to fulfill commandments?

_____

_____

3. What are the advantages and disadvantages of living as a Jew in your community?

_____

_____

RAMBAM'S TRAVELS

Here is a map of the area surrounding the Mediterranean Sea.
Trace Rambam's travels on this map. Write the dates in which he lived in each place.

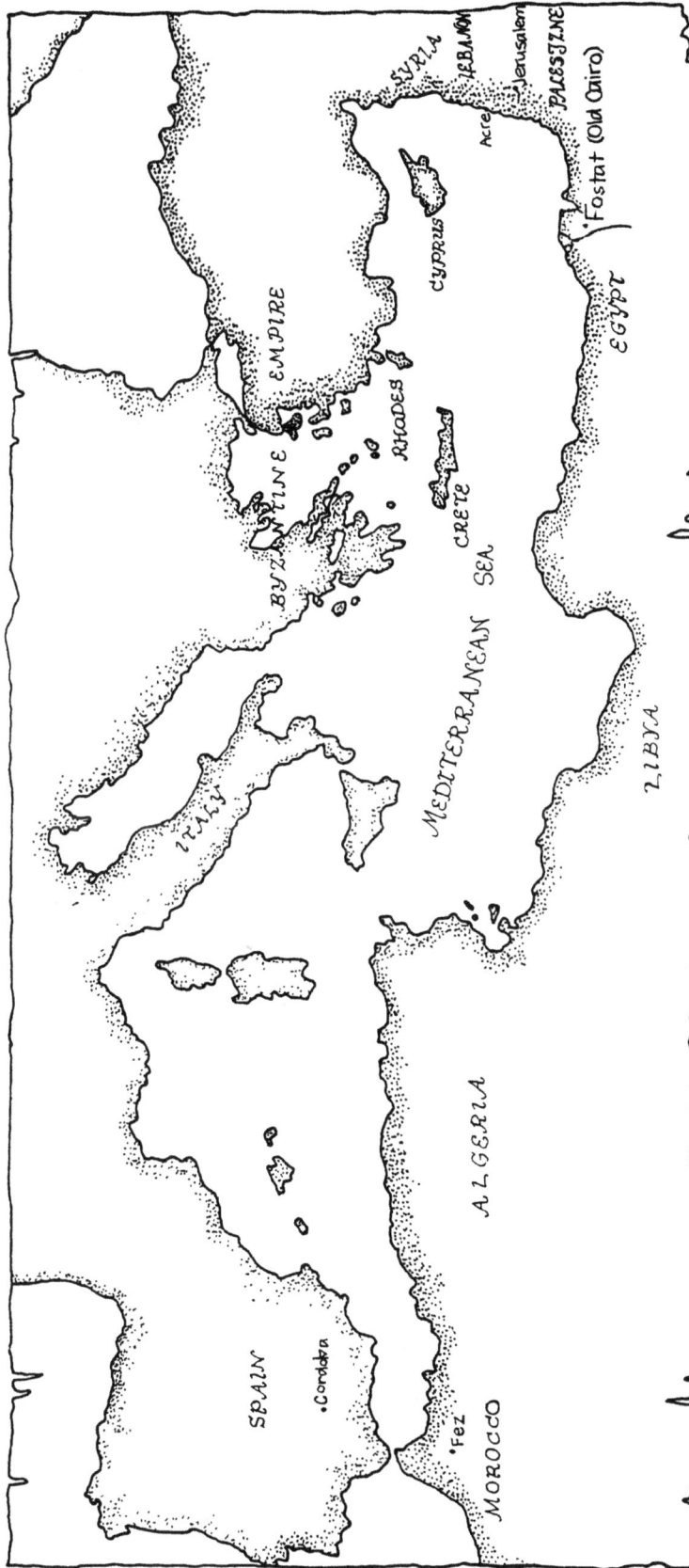

SPAIN
•Cordoba

MOROCCO
•Fez

ALGERIA

LIBYA

ITALY

BYZANTINE EMPIRE

RHODES

CRETE

MEDITERRANEAN SEA

CYPRUS

SYRIA

LEBANON

Acre

Jerusalem

PALESTINE

EGYPT

•Fostat (Old Cairo)

David's Travels

Here is a map of the area travelled by people who took the route to India.

Circle the place that David, Rambam's brother, reached. Mark with an X the country he wanted to reach.

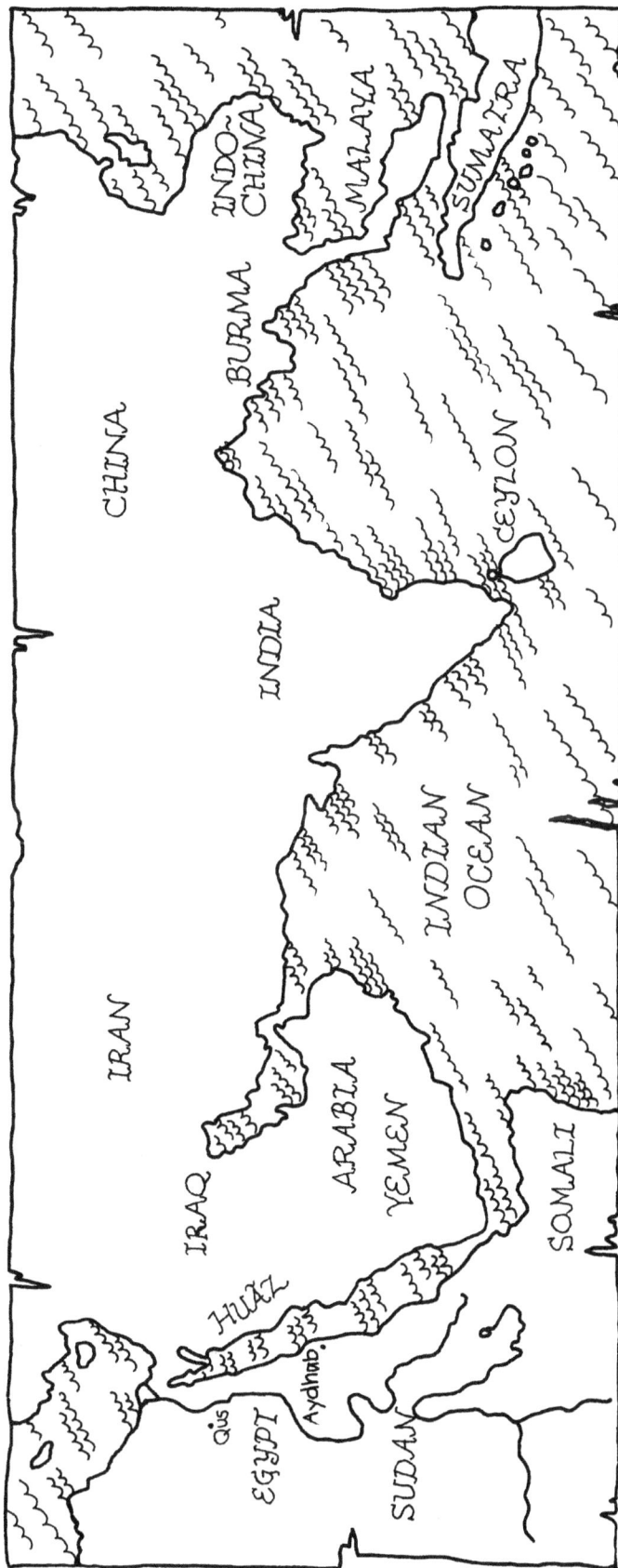

CHINA

IRAN

IRAQ

HIJAZ

Qūs

Aydhab.

EGYPT

SUDAN

ARABIA

YEMEN

SOMALI

INDIA

INDIAN OCEAN

BURMA

INDO-CHINA

MALAYA

SUMATRA

CEYLON

dates to remember

H ere are some years in the life of Moses Maimonides. Write why they are important.

1135 _____

1148 _____

1158 _____

1160 _____

1165 _____

1168 _____

1169 _____

1178 _____

1204 _____

INTRODUCTION

_____
_____
_____
_____
_____
_____
_____
_____
_____
_____
_____
_____

BY_____

Suppose Maimonides' famous works were being re-published in one large volume and you were asked to write the introduction in the front of the book. Explain why Maimonides wrote each work. Tell why Maimonides' writing is still important today. Here are some questions to help you:

1. Why did Maimonides write an Arabic commentary on the Mishnah?

2. Why did Maimonides write the _Guide for the Perplexed_? What language was it written in? Why?

3. Why did Maimonides write the _Mishneh Torah_? What language was it written in? Why?

4. What else did Maimonides write? Why?

For more help, look at some of the introductions that Maimonides wrote for his works.

time machine

Tune your Time Machine to one of the following situations by circling the number of the event you have chosen. Write about what you see happening.

Circle the number of the situation you have chosen.

1. A Jew comes to Maimon with a problem, and Moshe overhears the conversation.

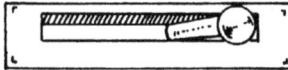

6. A Jewish tax collector comes to the house of a Jew who did not pay his taxes.

2. Moshe tells his mother about a difficult day at school.

4. The last conversation of Moshe and his brother David.

7. Maimonides treats the sultan for a headache.

3. A Jewish family discusses whether to leave Córdoba or convert to Islam after the Almohad conquest.

5. Rambam's wife attempts to console him after the death of his brother.

8. Maimonides explains to his son why he wrote the *Mishneh Torah* and *Moreh Nevuchim*.

Draw a picture of what you see in the space below.
Write about it on a separate piece of paper.

unit

2

talmud
torah

13

laws dealing with educat

Answer the questions below comparing laws about educat in
in the U.S. today and in Rambam's society.

	U.S. Today	Rambam's Socie
1. Who is obligated to study, and at what age ?		
2. Where do they study?		
3. Why is it important to study?		

4. The most important difference between the Jewish view of study (as practiced in
Rambam's society) and American ideas about study is:

_____

_____

_____

_____ Legal seal of
(Your commentator name)

If you were a teacher in Rambam's time...

Answer the questions below as if you were a teacher in Rambam's time.

... What would your qualifications include?

_____
_____
_____
_____
_____

... What would you be expected to do if your students don't understand?

_____
_____
_____
_____
_____

... How would your actions effect your students?

_____
_____
_____
_____

... Could you hit your students?

_____
_____
_____
_____

If you were a student in Rambam's time...

Answer the questions below as if you were a student in Rambam's time.

... At what age would you start school?

_____

_____

_____

... What would you do when your teacher walked into the classroom? What would you call your teacher?

_____

_____

_____

... What days would you go to school?

_____

_____

_____

_____

... What would you do if you didn't understand what your teacher was saying?

_____

_____

_____

_____

... When would you be allowed to ask your teacher a question?

_____

_____

_____

_____

16   *TALMUD TORAH: LESSON THREE*

RAMBAM REACTS

If Rambam found himself in one of these situations, how would he react?
Choose one of the situations below, and answer in the space provided.

1. A party at which people are sitting around talking about how they are so busy earning a living that they don't have time to open a book.

2. A classroom in which the teacher is screaming at a child who's slow to understand a lesson. "You stupid clod, I've explained this twice already and you still don't understand. What's wrong with you?"

3. In a small town with a few children, participants in a town meeting argue against the establishment of a local school.

4. A classroom in which the students in the back row are making paper airplanes and throwing them at each other.

5. A retirement home in Florida in which people are complaining that now that they're no longer working, they feel useless and see no meaning in their lives, playing golf, spending time in conversation.

ethical will

You've read the ethical will of Judah Ibn Tibbon in which he gives his son, Samuel,
guidelines for living. Your parents can use this page to write an ethical will for you.
If your parents are unable to write an ethical will for you,
imagine you are a parent and write an ethical will.

_____

_____

_____

_____

_____

_____

_____

_____

_____

_____

_____

_____

_____

_____

_____

_____

_____

illuminated manuscript

Trace any of the patterns below to create your own illuminated frontispiece
(front page) for any of Rambam's works.

אבבגד זסעפפ
הוזחתט ך.צצק
י.בכך ר.ש.ד.
למסנ שתתו

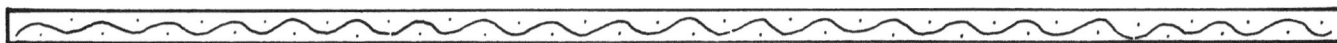

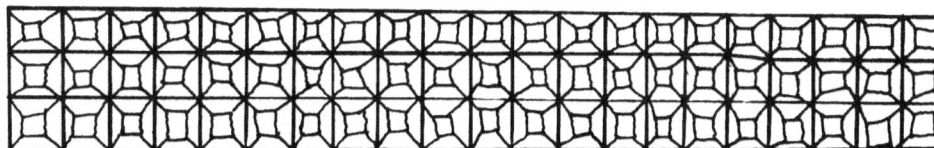

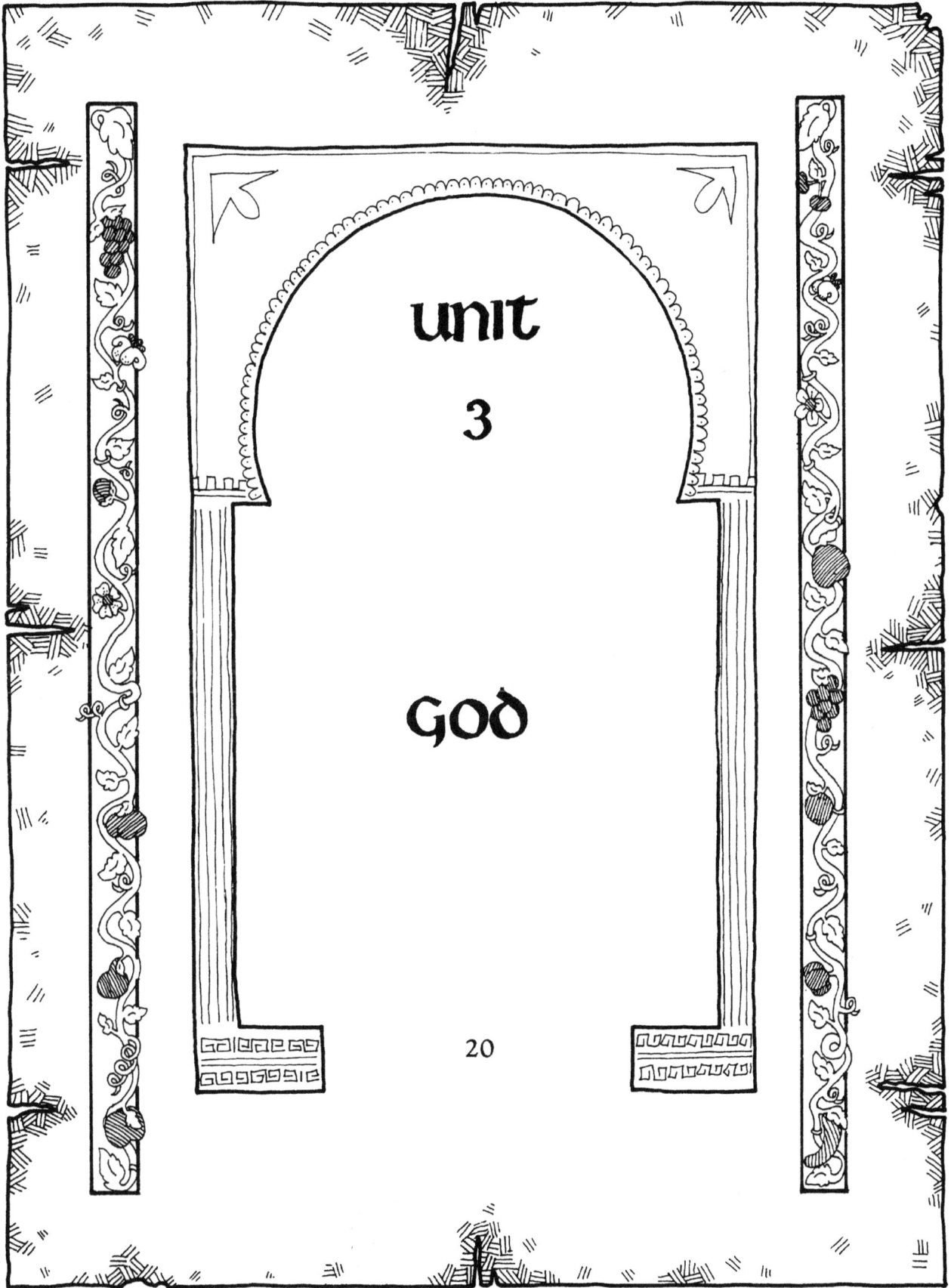

unit
3

god

philosophical argument for the existence of god

Pretend that you are a medieval philosopher arguing for the existence of God. Choose any natural phenomenon and write your own *teleological* or *cosmological* argument on the journal page below.

from the journal of _____

(Your medieval rabbi name here)

in other words 1

Here is Judah Halevi's poem in the original Hebrew and also translated into English.
On the next page, take the translation one step further.
Translate the poetic English into prose.

Lord, where shall I find Thee?
High and hidden is Thy place;
And where shall I not find Thee?
The world is full of Thy glory.

I have sought Thy nearness,
With all my heart have I called Thee
And going out to meet Thee
I found Thee coming toward me.

יָהּ אָנָא אֶמְצָאֲךָ? מְקוֹמְךָ נַעֲלָה וְנֶעְלָם!
וְאָנָא לֹא אֶמְצָאֲךָ? כְּבוֹדְךָ מָלֵא עוֹלָם!
דָּרַשְׁתִּי קִרְבָתְךָ, בְּכָל לִבִּי קְרָאתִיךָ
וּבְצֵאתִי לִקְרָאתְךָ-לִקְרָאתִי מְצָאתִיךָ

in other words 1

Write your translation of Judah Halevi's poem in the space below.

_____ , translator

my personal experience

Write about a way you can "go out to meet God."
(What will you do? What do you think the outcome will be?
How will the experience affect you?)

signed, _____

a medieval mystery

Identify each of the men below by carefully analyzing their answers.

Q. Do you believe in God?

a. Yes

Q. Do you believe in God?

a. Yes

Q. Explain your belief.

a. God is the creator of the Universe! How can anyone who is intelligent imagine that the places, sizes, and numbers of the stars, etc. occur by chance? Such things are done by a purposeful Being.

Q. Explain your belief.

a. I feel God's presence. God led my people out of Egypt with signs and miracles. That is convincing for me.... uninterrupted tradition!

Do you know who is who? Write your answer below, then fill in the two captions on the following page.

This man's
identity is: _____

This man's
identity is: _____ ____

a medieval mystery

Q. How do you act to imitate God?

a. _____
_____
_____
_____
_____
_____
_____
_____
_____
_____
_____
_____
_____

Q. How do you act to imitate (or "go out to meet") God?

a. _____
_____
_____
_____
_____
_____
_____
_____
_____
_____
_____
_____
_____
_____

What do you think about Rambam's way of thinking? Of Judah Halevi's way of thinking?
Answer on a separate sheet of paper.

GOD: LESSON FOUR

in other words 2

Here is Judah Halevi's poem in the original Hebrew and also translated into English.
On the next page, take the translation one step further. Translate
the poetic English into prose.

MY HEART IS IN THE EAST

My heart is in the East and I in the
    uttermost west—[1]
How can I find savour in food? How shall it
    be sweet to me?
How shall I render my vows and my bonds,
    while yet
Zion lieth beneath the fetter[2] of *Edom*,[3] and I in
    Arab chains?
A light thing would it seem to me to leave all
    the good things of Spain—
Seeing how precious in mine eyes it is to behold
    the dust of the desolate sanctuary.

1. taste

2. chains

3. area of Christian crusades

לִבִּי בְמִזְרָח

לִבִּי בְמִזְרָח וְאָנֹכִי בְּסוֹף מַעֲרָב

אֵיךְ אֶטְעֲמָה אֵת אֲשֶׁר־אֹכַל וְאֵיךְ יֶעֱרָב?

אֵיכָה אֲשַׁלֵּם נְדָרַי וֶעֱסָרַי בְּעוֹד

צִיּוֹן בְּחֶבֶל אֱדוֹם וַאֲנִי בְּכֶבֶל עֲרָב?

יֵקַל בְּעֵינַי עֲזֹב כָּל־טוּב סְפָרַד כְּמוֹ

יֵקַר בְּעֵינַי רְאוֹת עַפְרוֹת דְּבִיר נֶחֱרָב.

Spain

Palestine

27

in other words 2

Write your translation of Judah Halevi's poem in the space below.

_____
_____
_____
_____
_____
_____
_____
_____
_____
_____
_____
_____
_____
_____
_____
_____
_____
_____
_____

_____ , translator

In your opinion

Suppose your family was making aliyah...

What would you be happy about?

Draw your face here:

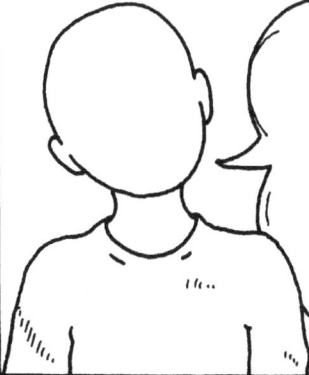

What would you be sad about?

Draw your face here:

How do your feelings compare to Judah Halevi's feelings?

personal puzzle

Solve this puzzle from the past. Begin at the arrow at the top of the outer ring. Go clockwise and read every other letter for *two* trips around each ring, following the arrow from one ring to the next.

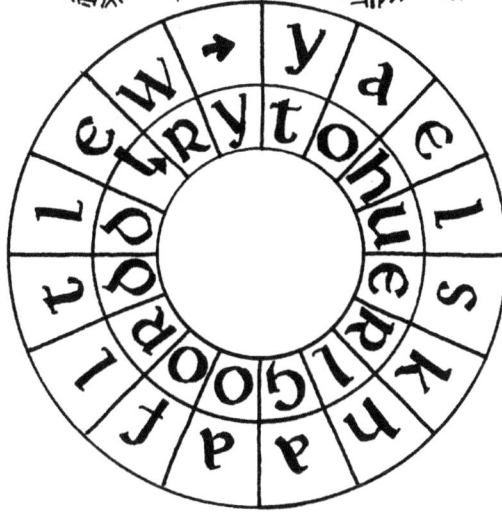

Answer: _____

According to R. Hama, how can a person do the above? _____

_____

_____

_____

_____

Tell of some other ways people can follow God: _____

_____

_____

_____

_____

(Letter ring puzzle from *Research Puzzles for Judaic Resources,* U. A. H. C.)

eight degrees of tzedakah

Below you see the Eight Degrees of Tzedakah, according to Rambam. Cut out along the solid lines and try to put the degrees in order from highest to lowest. Then read the section of the *Mishneh Torah* to see if you found the proper order.

Gives less money to the poor person than he should, but gives willingly.	Gives unwillingly.
Gives money anonymously, but knows to whom is giving.	Gives money anonymously and poor person receives anonymously.
Gives money to poor person after he is asked to.	Helps the poor to help themselves.
Giver of money is known, but receiver remains anonymous.	Gives money to poor person before he is asked.

unit
4

ta'amei
hamitzvot

anthropologist report

NAME:_____

I have observed a day in the life of Abu Yaakob Yosef, and have seen the following Moslem influences:

_____

_____

_____

_____

I have also observed these Jewish practices:

_____

_____

_____

_____

CROSSWORD PUZZLE

ACROSS:

1. What was Abu Yaakob Yosef's profession?

2. This was a popular game in medieval Spain.

3. What mitzvah did the pious merchant who died perform?

4. Moslems, Jews, and Christians shared this house.

5. How many utensils did Abu Yaakob Yosef's family use when they ate?

12. The people in Abu Yaakob Yosef's synagogue didn't need prayer books because they _____ the prayers by heart.

DOWN:

1. It was considered immodest for women to go here.

6. _____ was difficult for merchants in medieval Spain.

7. What did Abu Yaakob Yosef's children do to the floor during dinner?

8. Besides Arabic grammar, this was studied in Jewish schools.

9. Abu Yaakob Josef was careful when buying this.

10. Did Abu Yaakob Yosef's taxes go to the Moslem government?

mitzvot wordsearch

The Jews of Toledo performed many mitzvot. Find eight mitzvot hidden in the word-search below. They are hidden horizontally, vertically, backwards and forwards.

```
O  B  S  E  R  V  E  S  H  A  B  B  A  T
R  U  A  T  E  I  N  S  U  K  K  A  H  O
H  A  I  N  K  N  D  O  I  E  F  A  T  N
F  R  D  N  T  B  L  M  B  S  E  R  O  F
A  O  M  P  N  D  H  W  H  G  R  D  E  V
O  N  O  S  H  E  L  P  E  D  P  O  O  R
M  H  R  S  A  I  D  K  A  D  D  I  S  H
F  G  N  I  R  I  N  Y  D  C  F  R  O  T
S  R  I  E  O  S  D  O  N  T  L  M  O  V
O  U  N  S  T  S  C  K  A  E  A  R  E  A
T  H  G  I  D  N  R  L  I  E  S  S  P  L
I  S  P  A  E  S  U  R  E  D  M  P  N  L
T  T  R  I  I  F  F  E  E  S  D  M  O  R
E  H  A  R  D  L  N  K  I  N  A  U  I  E
O  E  Y  S  U  I  A  D  E  E  H  E  S  O
T  K  E  P  T  K  O  S  H  E  R  L  E  H
H  O  R  U  S  M  E  L  U  Y  H  N  B  D
O  P  S  O  H  Y  A  S  R  I  S  M  O  T
```

Jewish American

What actions do we Jews in America today have in common with our non-Jewish neighbors?

_____

_____

_____

_____

What actions do we Jews in America have that are uniquely Jewish?

_____

_____

_____

_____

FOR DISCUSSION:

1. What do we have in common with the Jews of Toledo?

2. Who (we or they) is more influenced by outside culture? Why?

time traveler

The time machine has been invented, and you have been chosen to travel to Toledo during Abu Yaakob Yosef's time. Your mission is to study the way Jews live, and report back to scientists in our time. You must act like a Spanish Jew so that the community will accept you.

Check the things listed below that you already know to do:

———— Eat Kosher food

———— Read Arabic books

———— Celebrate Sukkot

———— Speak to Moslem friends

———— Play chess

———— Say Kiddush and birkhat hamazon

———— Wear Moslem clothing

———— Eat Moslem-style

———— Wash your hands and feet before entering the synagogue

List other things you would have to learn.

_____

_____

_____

_____

_____

_____

_____

_____

_____

_____

moslem court in medieval spain

Below is a picture of a Moslem court in medieval Spain. On a separate sheet of paper, write a story about what you see happening.

how would you feel?

Pick one of the following situations and write how you would
feel if you were the person involved.

1. You are Abu Yaakob Yosef's daughter. What do you do each day? What do you expect to do when you grow up? What do you like about your situation? What do you dislike about your situation?

_____

_____

_____

_____

_____

2. You are Abu Yaakob Yosef's son. What do you do each day? What do you expect to do when you grow up? What do you like about your situation? What do you dislike about your situation?

_____

_____

_____

_____

_____

scenes from the kuzari

Summarize the selection from the *Kuzari* by filling in the missing parts in the following conversation between the Rabbi and the King of the Khazars.

TA'AMEI HAMITZVOT: LESSON FOUR

mitzvah machine 1

Fill in the missing data on the Mitzvah Machine. Then go back and place
a star next to the reasons that are most meaningful to you.

כַּשְׁרוּת

My reasons:

_____
_____
_____
_____
_____
_____
_____
_____
_____
_____
_____

Class reasons:

_____
_____
_____
_____
_____
_____
_____
_____
_____
_____
_____

Rambam's reasons:

_____
_____
_____
_____
_____
_____
_____
_____
_____
_____
_____

Halevi's reasons:

_____
_____
_____
_____
_____
_____
_____
_____
_____

Dresner's reasons:

_____
_____
_____
_____
_____
_____
_____
_____
_____
_____
_____

mitzvah machine 2

Fill in the missing data on the Mitzvah Machine. Then go back and place
a star next to the reasons that are most meaningful to you.

שַׁבָּת	My reasons:	Class reasons:

Rambam's reasons:	Halevi's reasons:	Dresner's reasons:

my mitzvah

Choose a mitzvah from the previous page concerning either כַּשְׁרוּת or שַׁבָּת. Draw a picture related to it in the space above. In three or four sentences explain why that mitzvah is the most meaningful to you.

_____

_____

_____

_____

_____

shabbat and the jews

"More than the Jews have preserved the Shabbat, the Shabbat has preserved the Jews."

- Ahad ha' Am

Explain how the following mitzvot, done on Shabbat, help preserve the Jewish people:

1. The mitzvah to refrain from work on Shabbat helps preserve the Jewish people because

_____

_____

_____

2. Going to synagogue on Shabbat helps preserve the Jewish people because _____

_____

_____

_____

3. The mitzvah of studying Torah on Shabbat helps preserve the Jewish people because

_____

_____

_____

List as many other mitzvot of Shabbat as you can in the space below.
How do these actions preserve the Jewish people?

_____

_____

_____

LOGIC OR EMOTION

I give the following reasons for observing the mitzvot of kashrut: Esthetics, to teach kindness, to remove us from idolatry, to teach us proper ideas about God.

I give the following reasons for observing the mitzvot of Shabbat: they bring us closer to God, they help preserve the Jewish people, they remind us of God as creator.

Judah Halevi	Rambam

1. Whose reasoning provides the more *logical* connection to God through mitzvot?

_____

Explain why you think so. _____

_____

_____

2. Whose reasoning provides the more *emotional* connection to God through mitzvot?

_____

Explain why you think so. _____

_____

_____

ta'amei hamitzvot
(reasons for the mitzvot)

Choose three mitzvot from among the following list. Cut them out, and paste them in the spaces on the next page. Then answer the questions, using the books your teacher has provided.

Blowing a shofar on Rosh Hashanah

Sitting in a sukkah on Sukkot

Fasting on Yom Kippur

Praising God after eating

Putting a mezzuzah on the door

Reciting the Shema each morning and evening

Shaking a lulav and etrog on Sukkot

ta'amei hamitzvot

1. What are the reasons for this mitzvah? _____

_____

2. According to whom? _____

_____

3. Which reason is most acceptable to you? _____

_____

_____ 4. Why? _____

1. What are the reasons for this mitzvah? _____

_____

2. According to whom? _____

_____

3. Which reason is most acceptable to you? _____

_____

_____ 4. Why? _____

1. What are the reasons for this mitzvah? _____

_____

2. According to whom? _____

_____

3. Which reason is most acceptable to you? _____

_____

_____ 4. Why? _____

unit
5

messianism

48

in the days of the mashiah

1. There will be a war against the Jews, but the Jews will win. Then Israel will return to its days of glory. The Temple will be rebuilt. All the Jews will return to Israel. The laws of nature will prevail, but people will spend their time in study.

2. The Mashiah will come after a terrible war in which the Jews will win and their enemies will be punished. Jews will return to the land of Israel. The dead will come alive again. There will be no disease or sadness. Everyone will be a prophet.

3. All people will be angels and live forever. The earth will bring forth garments already woven and bread already baked. Many other miraculous things will happen.

4. Write about how you think it will be when the Mashiah comes. Draw a picture to illustrate your ideas.

mishneh torah crossword

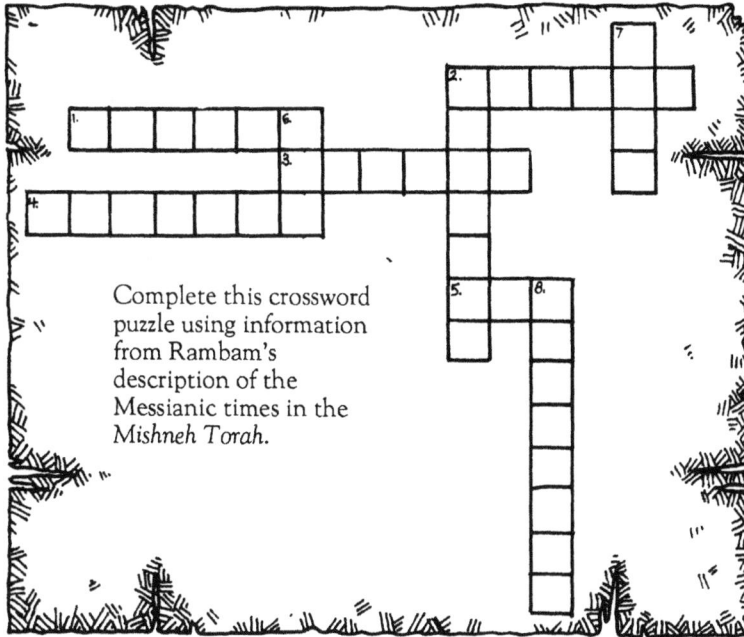

Complete this crossword puzzle using information from Rambam's description of the Messianic times in the *Mishneh Torah*.

ACROSS:

1. The _____ will be rebuilt when the Mashiaḥ comes.

2. There will be neither _____ nor war.

3. In the days of the Mashiaḥ the laws of _____ will not be set aside.

4. You will know that the person who claims to be Mashiaḥ is truly so because he will _____.

5. The Messianic era will begin with the war of _____ and Magog.

DOWN:

2. Israel should be delivered from serving _____ powers.

6. No one should spend much time on calculating the _____.

7. The goal of the Messianic era will be to _____ the Lord.

8. The dispersed of Israel will be _____.

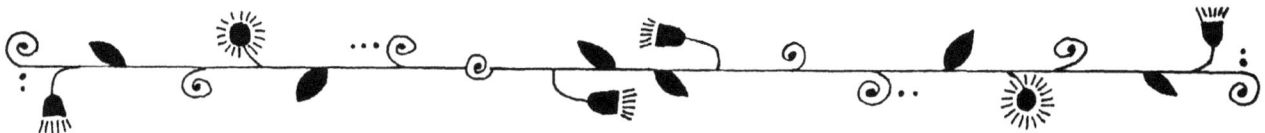

RAMBAM REACTS AGAIN

Pretend that Rambam read your ideas about how it will be when the Mashiaḥ comes.
Write his reaction in the bubble below.

Here is how your ideas about when the Mashiaḥ comes compare to mine:

_____

_____

_____

_____

_____

_____

_____

_____

_____

_____

_____

_____

_____

_____

_____

_____

_____

_____

THE MEET THE MINDS SHOW

This evening Rita Book will interview Rabbi Moses ben Maimon, whom you may know as Rambam...

Answer the questions below as you think Rambam would.

1. In your selection from the *Mishneh Torah* about the Mashiaḥ, why did you say, "Let no one think that in the days of the Mashiaḥ any of the laws of nature will be set aside...?"

_____

_____

2. Why was Bar Kokhba accepted as the Mashiaḥ by Rabbi Akiva and other great sages?

_____

_____

3. If you had lived then, would you have accepted him? Why or why not?

_____

_____

4. How do your beliefs about Messianic times differ from Christian beliefs?

_____

_____

_____

Use a separate piece of paper if you need more room.

set it straight

This ancient document telling Saadiah Gaon's views of Messianic times was torn and then put back together incorrectly. Fix it by listing in order the events that will happen before Mashiah ben David appears. Number from 1 to 8 below.

_____ Gog and Magog will fight against the Jews and be defeated.

_____ Nations of the world will convert to Judaism.

_____ Everyone will be a prophet, people will serve God with their whole hearts, there will be no disease or sadness.

_____ Jews will be brought to the land of Israel.

_____ The enemies of Israel will be defeated.

_____ Mashiah ben David will capture Jerusalem.

_____ There will be disasters and Jews will repent.

_____ Temple will be rebuilt.

factfinder's clipboard

Compare Maimonides' ideas about the Messianic age to those of Saadiah Gaon.
Fill in the chart below with the information you have found.

	Maimonides	Saadiah Gaon
What are the characteristics of the Mashiaḥ?		
What is the sequence of events leading up to the Messianic age?		
How will the lives of Jews change when the Mashiaḥ comes?		
How will the lives of non-Jews change when the Mashiaḥ comes?		

rambam-saadiah Gaon

Which beliefs about Messianic Times belong to Rambam and which belong to Saadiah Gaon?
Draw a line connecting the sentences below to a person who said each one.
Some beliefs apply to both men.

The enemies of Israel will be punished by fire and sulfur, by the sword, by the disintegration of their bones, and by being wounded in other ways.

There will be neither famine nor war, neither jealousy nor strife. Blessings will be abundant, comforts within reach of all.

The Mashiaḥ will not perform signs or wonders.

The laws of nature will not be set aside.

The Sages and Prophets did not long for the days of the Mashiaḥ so that Israel would be exalted by the nations.

The dead will be resurrected.

The nations of the world will carry Jews to Jerusalem on horses, on mules, or on their shoulders.

The Temple will be rebuilt.

Nations of the world will convert to Judaism.

Rambam

Saadiah Gaon

55

Rambam's false mashiah Detector

Could any of these false Mashiahs have fooled Rambam? Run them through this False Mashiah Detector and find out. Tell why each one could or could not have fooled Rambam.

Bar Kokhba _____   Moses al-Dari _____

Abu Isa _____   Ibn Aryeh _____

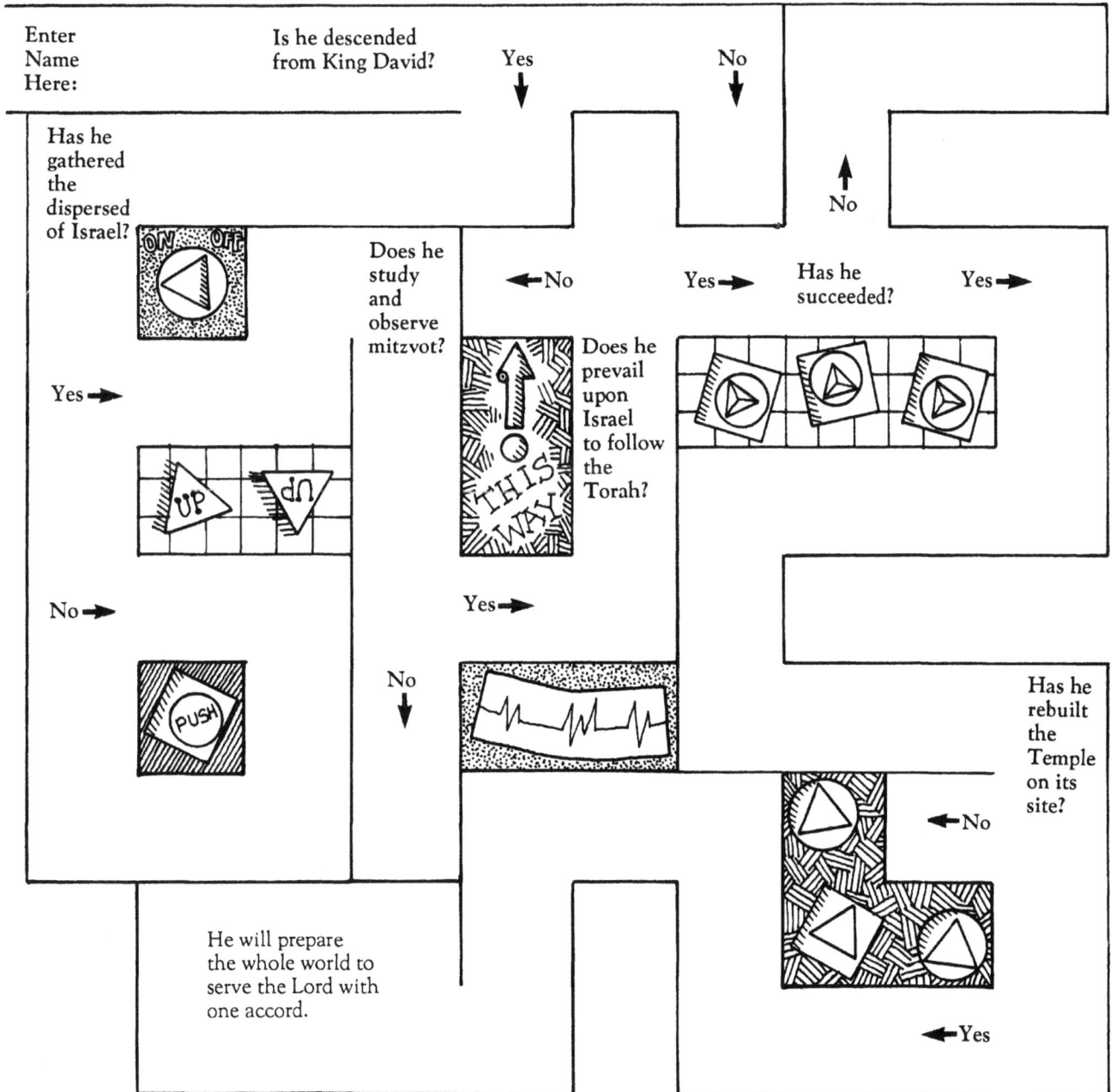

Enter Name Here:

Is he descended from King David?   Yes   No

Has he gathered the dispersed of Israel?

ON   OFF

Does he study and observe mitzvot?

←No   Yes →   Has he succeeded?   Yes →

No

Yes →

Does he prevail upon Israel to follow the Torah?

UP   UP

THIS WAY

Has he rebuilt the Temple on its site?

Yes →

No →

No

He will prepare the whole world to serve the Lord with one accord.

PUSH

←No

←Yes

www.ingramcontent.com/pod-product-compliance
Lightning Source LLC
Chambersburg PA
CBHW081214020426
42331CB00012B/3027